Communion of Saints

Communion of Saints

Susan L. Miller

POEMS

PARACLETE PRESS
BREWSTER, MASSACHUSETTS

2017 First Printing

Communion of Saints: Poems

Copyright © 2017 by Susan L. Miller

ISBN 978-1-61261-858-6

I Believe In You; Words and Music by Neil Young. Copyright (c) 1970 by Broken Arrow Music Corporation. Copyright Renewed. All Rights Reserved. Used by Permission. Reprinted by Permission of Hal Leonard LLC.

The Paraclete Press name and logo (dove on cross) are trademarks of Paraclete Press, Inc.

Library of Congress Cataloging-in-Publication Data

Names: Miller, Susan L., 1974- author.
Title: Communion of saints / Susan L. Miller.
Description: Brewster, Massachusetts : Paraclete Press, [2017]
Identifiers: LCCN 2016047155 | ISBN 9781612618586 (paperback)
Subjects: | BISAC: POETRY / Inspirational & Religious. | RELIGION / Christian
    Theology / General. | RELIGION / Christian Life / Prayer.
Classification: LCC PS3613.I5557 A6 2017 | DDC 811/.6--dc23
LC record available at https://lccn.loc.gov/2016047155

10 9 8 7 6 5 4 3 2 1

Published by Paraclete Press
Brewster, Massachusetts
www.paracletepress.com

Printed in the United States of America

For Josh

and in memory of
+Charles William "Flynn" Hirsch

Table of Contents

III. LOVE

IV. PAX ET BONUM

Foreword

My friend Anne, a Tibetan Buddhist, posts hotly colored images of deities and demigods on the walls of the room where she writes—just a few from the dazzling array of her collection, a huge celestial cast. Some are radiant, some tender, some poised in a cool regard for nothing we can see. The fierce ones can be unnerving, with their necklaces of skulls and their teeth dripping blood. I began to feel more friendly toward these when Anne described the images as visual representations of states of consciousness, pictures one might contemplate to access a quality of mind or heart in oneself. Just as we need to find our steadfastness sometimes, or to more fully inhabit our kindness, so we may suffer without our ferocity, without embodying that which cuts loose, or dissolves old associations, and goes striding fearlessly into the future.

Something like this idea seems to me to inform Susan Miller's understanding of the saints, whose lives and example resonate through this collection with remarkable power. We are all called to be saints, the Church teaches, and we form a "communion" with those who have gone before, those who stand with us, and those who are yet to come. For Miller the saints seem both their historical or legendary selves and archetypes or emblems. Their energetic presence is to be found among friends and colleagues, neighbors and parish-members. It's an especially lovely way of thinking about history, and the continuing presence of grace in community, in the works of the living.

And, since these are poems about the living—parents, theologians, teachers, parishioners, artists, writers, housekeepers, nurses, nuns, babies in a neonatal intensive care unit—they are poems of struggle, of what the poet has elsewhere called "the arduous work of being human." This book's revelatory strategy is to place these very real lives into relation with the saints, and in this way Miller's tender attention lifts people she knows and loves into another sort of light, not an elevation that erases flaws or human failings, but a way of seeing, within the daily, vectors of grace.

Miller's book is marvelously populated, and both failings and grace are reflected everywhere in these portraits. There are studies of what might be personal saints of Miller's, Flannery O'Connor and Nina Simone, Gwendolyn Brooks, Gerard Manley Hopkins, brilliant makers who spun art from trouble. The poet finds herself mirrored in the lives of St. Edith Stein, St. Agatha, and St. John of the Cross. And there are Miller's most densely structured poems, "double portraits" in which the speaker sees in or behind one of her friends the shadow form of a saint. These poems present a dyad—an elder poet in her garden, for instance, and St. Fiacre, the patron saint of gardeners—but in truth they're three-way studies, since their speaker is very much onstage; it's she who sees for us the tender gesture of an almost impossibly tiny flower held in the older writer's hand.

Surveyors use a process of triangulation to identify their location. Miller's poems do something like this too: here's Chayo, cooking chayote soup and talking about her son who should have died and didn't, and here's St. Jude, patron of lost causes, and here is the speaker in "Portrait of Chayo as St. Jude Thaddeus", being instructed by cook and saint both that no cause is entirely lost: devotion, faith, or ingenuity may yet rescue both soup and sons. It takes these three characters to bring this poem to life, to lend depth and resonance to the scene.

If poems are to resemble the world in which we find ourselves they must leave room for uncertainty, for interactions whose shadows and depths we may never understand. "Diptych of Two Charleses as St. Irene and St. Sebastian" is a compelling illustration of the principle that the poetry of faith is not necessarily, or even usually, a poem of certainty. The poem introduces us to two gay men, one a friend of the speaker's. She joins him for dinner in his apartment and hears the story of an old friend of his, a man who shares his first name. "Friend" seems too mild a word; the poem doesn't tell us whether the Charleses were ever lovers, but it does make clear that one has been St. Sebastian, the adventurer, the wilder spirit whose racked body is so often the subject of beautiful display, while the other has played the role of St. Irene, comforter, protector who could not protect. Charles One describes Charles Two as in terrible shape, but when the two men and our speaker meet, to visit a Kandinsky show at the Guggenheim, he seems fine. The three enjoy the exhibit until they're stopped in their progress by a masterwork, described in this way:

> crowning jewel of the exhibition: Several Circles,
> a map of the universe in blues, pinks, black, red, gold,
> and purple. At its center, the largest circle deepens to a
> dark
> iris, like an eye that enters the viewer's gaze. I say so.

If the speaker has been a kind of saint, for a moment, smoothing the waters between these two men, enabling all three to enjoy the outing, then suddenly Kandinsky seems one too, since he's punctured the moment with a gaze that seems to "enter the viewer's gaze." The painting is so startlingly alive that it seems, as only the greatest art does, to be looking at us.

The poem leaves the three friends rapt in study of the picture:

> And the three
> of us sink into contemplation of the colors: within us,
> the superimposed circles rising and floating, trapped
> beneath our ribs like wounds that heal themselves.

They have been given a gift, brought together in contemplation of an image of color in harmony, of color that can heal. Kandinsky thought of his brilliantly colored abstractions as expressions of psychic states, and thought that color communicated directly to the human soul. But what a mysterious gift his painting has brought to these three. It seems, by becoming an eye itself and entering the viewers' collective gaze, to offer a sort of renewal on a frigid winter day. He who believes the other needs care, and he the adventurer who may or may not need rescue, and she who wants to be a good friend, to be of use—all are suspended a moment, caught up in the clear and reassuring light that emanates from the canvas. Just why these three characters need a healing, or to what degree, outside this moment, this bit of grace may avail, the poem doesn't say. It brings us right to the moment where, as in a Flannery O'Connor story, a character might choose grace, or be chosen by it.

The book comes to rest with a series of poems concerning St. Francis, marking his humility and affection for animal life, and exploring the poet's pilgrimage to Assisi in search of confirmation, vision, some disruptive sign. I'd suggest that the final poem is such a sign. By employing the second person, Miller fuses both herself and her reader with the despised and homeless creature. Miller's wolf is the abject self without faith, without hope of receiving care or grace, or faith in some sustaining love. But this wolf does learn to receive charity from the hand of St. Francis, because it has been so terribly hungry, and because Francis does not strike. The wolf allows Francis to lead him or her into community, into a new possibility: a relation founded on love. What's offered is a complete revision of the world the wolf has known. Could the creature, or any of us, be one who'd be

> fed at any door you pass through,
> beloved and belonging. Would you
>
> call it a miracle if you knew
> that wherever you went,
> someone provided for you?

Every wanderer has felt lost, every abject soul has believed we'll never be "beloved and belonging." The wolf stands for all of us who have the opportunity to believe that a benevolence is there for us, a communion of saints we could attempt, in our wolfish or human ways, to join. I imagine it's no accident that this surprising and moving book begins with a "manual for would-be saints" and ends with a ruined, heartbroken wolf learning to be loved. To become a saint, the lesson might be, it is necessary to enter completely into one's abjection, and then to give oneself over completely to what might provide for your hunger.

Mark Doty
April, 2016

Manual for the Would-Be Saint

The first principle: Do no harm.
The second: The air calls us home.
Third, we must fill the bowls of others
before we drain our own wells dry.
The fourth is the dark night; the fifth
a subtle scent of smoke and pine.
The sixth is awareness of our duties,
the burnt offering of our own pride.
Seventh, we learn to pray without ceasing.
Eighth, we learn to sense while praying.
The ninth takes time: it is to discover
what inside the seed makes the seed increase.
The tenth brings sorrow, the eleventh light.
The twelfth we reflect on the Apostles,
their flame-lit faces turned toward us or away.
The thirteenth, we practice forgiving Judas.
The fourteenth, we love Judas as ourselves.
The fifteenth is a day of feasting; the sixteenth
is a day of ash. Seventeenth, we watch and wait.
Eighteenth, we enter the stranger's city
at the mercy of the stranger's hand.
Nineteenth, love flees the body,
and the spirit leaves its husk. And suddenly
the numbers do not matter: nothing that is matter
matters anymore: all is burned, all is born,
all is carried away in the wind.

I.

FAITH

A Vision

Last night I dreamed the church in winter.
Crowds of people filled the pews, laden
with armloads of roses and larkspur,
each with a tray of lit candles. St. Clare
loosened all her blonde hair in a pew
in the front of the sanctuary, and I knew
St. Francis nestled between friends somewhere.
The priest told us *In this dark hour of the year*
we light candles to dispel the vision of evil,
which shadows us whenever we forget to turn
towards the light. Directly I could feel
beside me the grey one on his ashen horse,
his face obscured under his tattered hood,
and felt the wind of his galloping, but
my candle's flame did not flicker.
You must make your own light, the Father said,
and as I raised my head I saw every man
and woman, every child, clean and naked,
brighter than the glow of a thousand candles.

Reading the Hours of
Catherine of Cleves/*I Believe in You*

On the A train, going downtown, the lights
flicker and dim, and the car wobbles
back and forth, shuttling at the speed of nausea.
In my seat, I bend with my elbows on my knees
and pray, though I don't know what I am praying for:
an end to the soot, the cold, the indignity
of slush crushed into dirty ice at the curb,
an end to illness rising like a cough
to shadow the kindness of my every word,
an end. I've been keeping Neil Young
on the Walkman, listening to his lament:
Now that you've made yourself love me, do you
think I can change it in a day? How can I
place you above me? And I wonder daily,
though John Donne and St. John and Gerard
and Thérèse believed, how can I know
what they thought was true is true?
It was so long ago...

And then I slide the Book of Hours from its blue
slipcover, the box built to keep it new,
and I open to a page where someone drew
(five hundred years ago) a dozen mussels, tiny, precise,
their dark lips ridged at the edge of their soft flesh,
just as they are in my dinner-bowl
when I steam them and eat them now.

Portrait of Chayo as
St. Jude Thaddeus

In a green apron, Chayo stirs chayote soup,
holding her palm taut so she can daub a taste there

to check the salt. Her skin doesn't feel the heat
though if I try the same I blister myself. She sings

while she chops chives into tiny rings
that float on the surface of the liquid.

When Clementina first told me about her, she taught me
in Spanish *riñones*, kidneys, because Chayo gave one

to her son, who almost died when his failed.
In Mexico City she pinned a bean-shaped charm

to the skirt of a statue. *Priests, I don't talk to much,*
she says, *but San Judas Tadeo, him I trust.*

I prayed to him to intercede, to heal my son. She lifts a copper bowl
down from the cabinet and hugs it

against her chest with both arms. *Now he works
as an engineer, and lives with his girlfriend.* She sets the bowl

on the counter, lifts a stack of plates onto
the wheeled cart she uses to set the table.

She wraps warm tortillas in a cloth, spoons salsa
into a shallow dish, fills the serving bowl

with pale green soup I watched her form
from three chayotes, a potato, and bouillon.

Above her the stove-light burns in its hood,
illuminating each loose strand of hair on her head.

Nothing, she tells me, *is a lost cause. This soup,
for example. If you cook it too long, add water and Norsuiza.*

If green beans turn dark, a little baking soda keeps them bright.
She smooths her hair and straightens her apron,

ready to serve. *And if you use a pressure cooker
for frijoles, they'll be perfect inside of half an hour.*

Portrait of Angela as St. Agnes

On Sunday, Angela slides into the pew beside me
saying, "Yesterday was my anniversary: eleven years

consecrated," and I puzzle. I know she isn't married,
have watched her bring her elderly mother to church,

serve communion barefoot, read from the pulpit
when our lector Eric's not present. She's always laughing,

a strong Italian scrape from deep in the chest, and when I came
to receive the sacred rites for the elect, she stood by

as Father crossed my palms with oil, the only person
I knew from church who wasn't also marked that day.

"I'm a Consecrated Virgin living in the world," she explains,
and shows me her gold wedding ring, shaped like a chain.

"The day of the ceremony, reporters crammed the cathedral:
no one believed that two virgins existed in Brooklyn.

The other's from Trinidad, and very serious. Her mother
told me *you've given my daughter the gift of laughter.*"

The day's reading, I Corinthians, says *An unmarried woman
or virgin is anxious about the things of the Lord,*

so that she may be holy in both body and spirit,
and I squeeze her hand, both of us chuckling.

After Mass, on the sidewalk, she jokes with the priest,
"Eleven years, and we've never had a fight."

"You and Jesus?" he asks. "My mother says He's the best
son-in-law in the world," she replies. She pulls on

her green scarf, fishes her keys, remarks that she's seeking
the Bishop's blessing for a residence for teenage girls

in our parish. "I visited him, and he said he would pray.
He thinks I'm a *nice woman*," she says, and laughs,

shaking her lamb's-wool curls. Three rosaries tangle
on the rearview mirror as she waves and drives away.

Portrait of Sister Carol as St. Cecilia

On a rainy Tuesday afternoon, I ring the bell
of the rectory to meet with Sister Carol,

who meets me standing in the hall
in her grey habit and black nurse's shoes. She brings

me around to the office, pointing out
the bulletin board where she has printed

YOU ARE THE CHILDREN OF LIGHT.
Beyond the door, we can hear grades K-8,

delighted at their afternoon break, their shouts
a lot of joyful noise. It's hard to hear the sister's voice,

on any day a humble tone, and here
between the rain and my deaf ear almost

inaudible, but when I ask how she found her vocation,
she ducks her face and shyly tells how her older brother

played his guitar for the choir where she followed.
"I still love those songs," she murmurs,

and I think of recent Sundays when she stood
among the children in the pew, barely taller, shushing

with whispers when the hymn began *Sing a new song
unto the Lord.* Surrounded by eager fidgeters

poking their brothers and sisters or diving to offer
envelopes to the collection basket, elbows

and crowns of heads and open mouths around her,
Sister Carol, married to God, was singing alleluia.

Self-portrait as St. Jerome

It is the red robe, the folds loose around the shoulders,
that marks him: the red robe, and the open book on the desk,
and the skull. Sometimes, a rough stone.

To hold that granite in hand is to know
that all knowledge could never match the scope
of one's own ignorance—the cranium empty, its eyes gone.

Mea culpa, mea culpa, mea maxima culpa. It is all
my fault, these faults of mine, a fractal pattern of cracks that deepen
into black chasms, black type on the page that I am too weary

to read. My blind hands smooth the pages. My dim
eyes gum the letters, which squirm between my eyelids
like tadpoles as I raise the stone again.

Portrait of Charles as St. Francis

Christmas Eve, a cold Friday,
after hours of cleaning and packing,
I called Charles to see if he would come over

for homemade chicken soup.
We had to eat it all; we'd leave the next morning
for Massachusetts, where Josh's mother

was still strong enough, despite her cancer,
to spend the day with family.
Our midnight Mass for the English-speaking

would be held at 8, choir music first,
then the procession of the infant Christ
to the crèche behind the altar.

Charles arrived with packages:
our wedding present, two years late
but no less sweet,

and a mysterious box taped and taped
with yellowed scraps of cellophane,
plus a plastic bag that held what looked like

another box. Cut open, it revealed
a crèche constructed from a peach flat,
its labels still visible under its bottom.

The other box, of course, was filled
with paper towels wrapped
around the Holy Family, German

figures painted in delicate pastels,
and a strange mismatched menagerie:
two glass birds, two camels,

the ass and the cow with one horn,
sheep flocked with fuzzy velvet,
some handsome angels. *This angel*

I won as an attendance prize at school, Charles said.
In the kitchen, Josh put on the soup,
then suggested, *Why don't you set it up*,

so I cleared the coffee table,
and down it went, the Easter grass
marked "Hay" laid in its floor,

the cotton marked "Snow"
on its roof. *I didn't know back then*
there wouldn't have been snow, Charles said.

He insisted the ox and ass be placed
beside the manger (*they kept him warm.*
The Bible says so.) When I set

the tallest angel in the back corner,
Charles rejoiced: *That's just*
where I used to put him, too!

I always wanted it to go to a family,
Charles said, as I set the cardboard manger
into the hay, and *Should we put Jesus*

in tonight? I asked. We all agreed
we should, and I laid him in a cotton wad
on his side, his sleeping face crowned

with a halo. Charles sat back on the couch
and surveyed the array: it seemed to suit,
and after our bowls of soup

we walked the six blocks to church,
where families had brought their own
images of Christ, icons arranged

in bassinets or boxes lined with cotton.
Look, the tiniest one! said Father,
lifting a doll the size of his palm.

Charles leaned over Josh in the pew. *Next year,*
he whispered, *we'll bring ours too.* And then we rose
to face the procession, the deacon bearing

the cross of San Damiano, both priests solemn,
and a boy lifting Jesus high
like Charles did one Christmas as a child.

Self-Portrait as St. John of the Cross

The world is small, a five-foot cell
with damp stone walls and not enough room to lie down.
And still I love you Lord though you have gone

from my thoughts like a hart that shoots
through the forest on the way to its own panicked future.
I have seen that deer. I know its pace,

the fleeing toward somewhere the world might offer grace.
I have been that deer. It sees only sky and feels
only the air howling in its ears, and then

darkness, and a sleep that does not rest
its sweat-chilled body trembling. My God
I know that even Christ

doubted his Father
for a moment, in his suffering, and cried out *My God
why hast thou forsaken me?* without

feeling your hand in his chest, that hand
that wraps itself around the human heart and presses gently
two times every second.

Portrait of Josh as St. Pascual Baylon

Every morning for years you knelt to pray the prayer
of St. Francis before the twenty-minute trudge to work,

through snow or in the rain, to unlock the kitchen,
kissing me goodbye at the door. Each day you came home

with a fresh cut, a burn, sometimes so slight you didn't
even bandage them, sometimes deep. I never knew

how your skin renewed itself. When the wounds
healed, you were still smooth to my touch.

I imagine you as a child in school, one of
the wild lambs, each day beginning with *Lord, make me*

an instrument of your peace, before you learned
to stay so quiet. Before the years turned you inward,

I know you ran headlong and unafraid, legs
pumping in the California sun. I've seen the gnarled

apple trees you ate from until you were sick of apples,
and I've seen the house you grew up in. You've kept

the handles carved in the shapes of bear and fox from
the chest of drawers, remembering the light of summer

afternoons, the warm interior of that house before
everything slowly cooled. You've always remembered

month and year, date and day, when I forget so easily.
Your angels throng around you; I imagine their

million eyes, their million wings shuddering,
a swarm of bright bees keeping the hovering shadows

at bay. Sometimes I cannot hear for all their singing.
I do not know if they always win. The years of suffering

are seared into your skin, but still each day you kneel
to pray in English and Hebrew, keeping the past

present with you, just as you leave the lids of jars
slightly loose, as you did for your mother

in the last years she was alive, so her arthritic hands
wouldn't hurt when she opened them.

Portrait of Father Santo as
St. Anthony of Padua

I. February

The Italian priest traveling with his relics
told us this story in a cliff-hanger style:
that St. Anthony's bones had been exhumed
so we could know how strange they were.
He died of dropsy, the little priest said,
but the most unusual thing was his kneecaps:
flattened, thinned, twice as wide as
a regular man's because he prayed
on his knees for hours every day.

At the front of the church, a huge gold
torso of St. Anthony raised one hand;
inside, the relics (a scapular bone?
part of an arm?) reminded me
that all we are, after we are, becomes
small and brown, as if time dyes our bodies
with tea and smoke. The priests
handed out prayer cards with an image
of the reliquary, green ones for Spanish,

blue for English, red for Italian. I took several,
knelt in front of the torso, held St. Anthony's
upraised hand in my hand and touched
the cards to the glass enclosure.
Uptown my 19-day-old daughter slept
inside her own clear isolette, so I prayed
not for anything I had lost (*O gentle and
loving St. Anthony who held the Christ child
in your arms*) but only not to lose her.

II. May

New mother that I was, I arranged confession
on a day I could walk to church and plan;
the baby in my arms made waiting difficult,

and nobody wanted to hear her cry
in the confession line. Father Santo
had made me tea, and gave a small

green apple to my daughter, which fell
and rolled around on the dining room floor
in the rectory. She kept wanting it,

reaching, so I bent down again and again
to retrieve it, and she'd palm it, then
drop it again. I don't remember

what I confessed—kicking the bottle
across the room after I dropped it,
cursing the hospital-grade pump,

probably cursing my husband, though
he'd done nothing wrong—but I remember
how thrilled she was to have the apple,

a little runty thing unfailing. Once
I had run out of sins to number,
Father Santo blessed me and held her—

his Goddaughter—while I collected
our things. And when I looked up,
Father was carrying her on his hip

(all six-pounds-seven-ounces of her,
the apple clutched in her two hands)
just like the foot-tall plaster statue behind him.

Mary Flannery O'Connor and Company

In Milledgeville, a Bird Sanctuary,
Flannery's mother Regina lets her choose

the forty peafowl—cocks and hens—
that drag their dun or dazzling plumes

across the bare-dirt yard. She's good
with birds, Miss Flannery, as proved

when as a girl she taught her favorite
chicken to walk backward as a stunt.

There's footage of it. Flannery
in stiff dress and patent-leather shoes

wary before the camera
coaches her hen to move

the opposite of what nature intended.
Its spurs go last in the dust, its talons wheeled

like the cut-out paper girl from a birthday card,
her four-legs'-wheel pinned on with a brad.

Birds are often better fun than humans,
smart and stubborn, boon

companions to the end, and they don't mind
if you're swollen, curt, or tired.

They don't mind much as long as corn
keeps coming from a feed-cup

as they rule their yard-wide domain,
a world where all have their place:

cocks shrieking loudly to corral the hens,
hens in comity, one chick pipping in a ring

to cap and rise from his shell
in damp and blinking wonder. It's her

world, too—from the bedroom window,
all she can see: the peacock spreads his crown

of green-and-purple jewels, six feet aloft
in the arms of a weathered tree.

II.

HOPE

Portrait of Mr. Menzies as
St. Rita of Cascia

After his stroke, for months, all I hear
of Mr. Menzies are stories his daughter carries
from the assisted living: he's improving,

he uses the wheelchair adeptly, he's ready
to return home. Then for a month, requests
for the priest. I write and mail letters, send him

prayer-cards of St. Francis, joke about my forays
into the lectorship, the Sunday I make everyone
do extra penance by reading the wrong section.

Finally, one Sunday I hear he's confessed
and received communion, and two weeks
later he's sitting in the pew, the back

of his head familiar, though shorn of
the small ponytail he used to wear. I gaze
through the homily at his curls of white hair.

When he rises for the Eucharist, returning
at once to his seat, I see his face in profile, skin
of his jaw translucent, veins visible under

his tan. A hard lump rises into my throat; I'm
so choked I worry I can't swallow the host.
But after the Mass, he greets me: "Thank you

for remembering me," he says, supported by
a three-footed cane. He asks about the bandage
on my ankle. "In case of a sprain, you chill

a quart bottle. Roll it over the ankle to make
the tendons return to their right places.
Then you tear a paper grocery bag in strips.

Soak them in vinegar, and wrap the foot. This
will bring the swelling down." I smile, remembering
the cough remedy he'd offered the week

I was baptized: coconut oil, lime juice, and salt,
which I warmed in a shot glass and drank.
Disgusting, but it worked. I thank him,

and we walk out together, me limping slightly,
him, tall and graceful in his good grey suit,
his cane barely grazing the floor.

Nina Simone Holds a Note

Late afternoon in a Paris apartment, she watches the sun
filter through the room. Dust motes float in the shy rays

like notes on a staff. She tucks a stray hair
into her bun, leans back into the cushions, her kimono sleeves

dragging. Remembers playing "Love Me or Leave Me"
in a high-necked dress to an all-white crowd when she was

twenty-five, posture erect, fingers sure on the keys
as they glided into a Bach riff, her eyes fixed and wide:

I'd rather be lonely than happy with somebody else, a phrase as
        snappy
as a lime in gin, as tart. She remembers that girl, young gifted

and black, already suspicious of polite admiration, striving
to show that she was perfect in form, sharp as the black keys. Not

smiling. Not there to please, but to stun. And after years
abroad, settled into this solitude absolutely, there is still

a sore sense in her of casting those notes into a sea
of indifference. Inside her a swamp of sore.

She tilts her head forward, hums a little, finds the spot
inside her chest where that deep voice resonates,

cradling the sound, the buzz of a chord that plucks the noise
of the empty street, the dust rising in the room, the withheld tears

of decades, and it bursts from her throat in a low lament,
scratched from her like the itch scratched from the scalp of a child

by a mother's gentle nails.

Portrait of Marie as St. Fiacre

Deep in afternoon, in your patio garden,
wind propels clematis and weeping willow,
thrashing limbs and flowers against the wall. We're
hopelessly rumpled.

You've been gaining strength through this wretched summer:
heat at 98, and the beat of hammers
jacking somewhere near so the floor is throbbing.
Strong as a hybrid,

you resisted death, though its weird confusions
left their mark on language you search to utter,
gone before you speak, and in urgent fashion
swapped for another.

Still, your tongue and mind are the ones I treasure:
fierce with wild desire under mild composure.
Eighty-nine, and here in the garden naming
flame-colored lilies,

vines and tendrils parting between your fingers,
you uncover blue in a twist of petals.
I have never seen such a tiny blossom.
You hand it over.

Here. Forget me not, you proclaim with relish.
Cupped inside my palm, the remembrance tickles,
light as wind, or light as our living mantle:
flown in a second.

Yet the wind stops, pausing before the evening
like you've said it does on consistent schedule.
Red and pink geraniums slow their bobbing,
restful and cheerful.

Now we've made our loop through the potted garden.
I'll go home to press your keepsake in paper,
and you, alone, return to your daily writing,
stubbornly thriving.

Portrait of Mark as St. Roch

In snow-crusted Chelsea, Mark has been ordered
to stay inside, favoring his sore eye,

though two weeks after surgery it barely shows
a rim of blood under the iris. After his many years

of nursing others, it's strange to see Mark
himself wounded, and though he says he's almost

back to normal, he admits that taking stairs
is precarious, and a cataract already forms

where the healthy lens used to be. I've come
to visit on a Thursday night, and Ned,

the golden retriever, 70 pounds
and eight months old, flings himself

against me, taking my scarf and sleeves
in his teeth. "I'm sorry," Mark says.

"It's fine. He's just in love," I laugh,
as the paws land on my shoulders again.

I stand with my arms extended. Mark
anoints me with Bitter Apple

head to toe, wrist to wrist, and then palms
my head, smoothing it into my hair,

which Ned takes into his mouth
in ecstasy. "Well, that's enough," Mark says,

and takes Ned by the collar to a chair,
then holds the dog between his thighs.

"Love is hard," he murmurs into Ned's muzzle,
their noses touching. "I hate love too."

At peace, the two are still, the shaggy head
tilted back to touch the grey one,

and I think how brave it is to love
through our broken bodies, in exile, in the cold,

to love even the dumb beasts we are
who only know enough to bring bread

to the one in pain.

Self-Portrait as St. Agatha

The computer screen maps the ghost
of my left breast, a blueprint transparent

so that I can see what's inside it:
a firework of white streaks enclosed

by the darker casing of its flesh. I ask
the radiation tech, a short Russian woman

with frosted hair, if all of them look
different. "As we get older, more and more

the same," she smiles. Her hands are firm
when she lays me on the glass plate,

careful to wipe the smeared surface
with Windex first, precise when finally

she lowers the top plate down. Other
women insist that this part hurts, but

when I was a child I learned to hate
a gentle touch, so being pressed flat

doesn't bother me. It seems honest
to grip hard, and I press my imperfect flesh

against this plate to offer up the proof
of my flaws and truths. I am not afraid

to be seen clearly. Poor bruised fruit,
these two are numbed, dumb, and innocent

though they have been pawed, mashed,
pinched and prodded, bumped,

and are now like someone's afternoon tea:
one lump or two. When I am sent

for the sonogram,
the handsome young tech who leads me in

tells me he will not perform that task.
"Oh. Not a breast man?" I ask.

Portrait of Ann as St. Stephen, Martyr

Behind her eyelids   white flashes
hailstones   or snappers

the sparks a chewed lifesaver
gives off   in the dark

or a flint-stone scratched
a pilot light   as if her skull

were filled with blue gas
head made of   blue glass

under the desk   on her side
in her windowless office

in the 15th hour   she can taste
tin   between her molars

the world a drum   and she's
the vibration inside   but she rises

to teach her second class
emerges   into the hallway

and the fluorescents strike   like a rock
flung   at the back of her head

Portrait of Evie as St. Martin de Porres

Late in the semester, on a Wednesday, we gather
among oil portraits of the founders
of the University. Walnut tables, upholstered chairs,

even the carpet's richer than those in our offices, our
beloved metal bookshelves and plastic-wood desks. Evie,
my colleague from down the hall, steps to the podium,

sleek in a black pantsuit and a heavy necklace
of brass and agate. She pushes her twisted locs
back from her face, raises her chin, and speaks.

Sixty faces train on her every gesture,
her hands rising to indicate a musical phrase
or punctuate a point. Her language slips, doubles,

*I was fragile   I was imported   I
was many   I give you back
what you have given me*

exposes the story beneath the story of a life
in negatives: don't. Can't. But
she does, and writes what she writes in order to say

I do and *will.* And she writes we, too: specific,
in every hue, the human family emerges and recedes
like the patterns behind eyelids when I close

my eyes. San Martin taught this kind of grace:
when called by royalty to heal the sick, he arrived,
knelt, and queried, *Why would a prince have need*

to call on a mulatto, a poor friar like me? Then,
knowing his powers exceeded anyone's
in that room, he laid his hand on the man's flesh

and healed him.

Portrait of E. as St. Thérèse of Lisieux

At lunch E. pulls aside her hair to show me
two blue dots tattooed just under her jaws,

on the sides of her throat. For radiation,
she says, the tattoos helped the techs

to line up the protective plates
in the same place every time. She felt

a lump in her neck one day, and the next,
real bad news. The radiation burned

so much that every minute in treatment
she called out from her mind, like a child,

St. Thérèse, heal me whole. Years later,
she still can't eat spices, tannins; even bubbles

in champagne abrade her fragile tongue. But
she is alive. One day she tells me, "I watched

the train pull in, stop, pull away, and realized
that for years I have been living in the moment,

uninterested in visiting the past, afraid
to hope for any future." Thérèse too

lived through a season of disbelief
in heaven, hiding behind her bed

in hollow prayer while the other nuns
thought her the most pious. It passed.

Good Friday, in the final year of her life,
when her own blood rose to her lips

for the first time, she rejoiced; she knew
that Christ had sent her a sign

of her end, in commemoration of his.
Riding to meet E. again, I watch the faces

on the subway and wonder how anyone
learns to face it. And yet

when we meet uptown to go to Mass,
E. greets me with "Look what I found!"

and hands me a Crayola printed *Dark Rose*
on its wrapper. "Isn't that a message?" I ask.

Self-Portrait as St. Christopher

In the streets of Prague, my friend Marcela
always left the map to me. *O captain my captain*
she called me, watching me trace our path

to some record store we meant to find, or a cafe
with cups of steamed chocolate and cream. I did
direct us well, my sense of the city formed

by the first day I spent there, just over my jet lag,
walking for seven hours until I found a station
from which I could return to the hostel,

The Horn and Hound, or whatever it was called.
By the time the others showed up I knew secrets
they would spend weeks discovering: that near

the edge of town there was Korean food,
that south of where we stayed the Dancing Building
kicked up its metaphorical heels. Parks

and bookstores, apricot pastries, the uneven
cobblestone streets became my bailiwick.
We wandered up the corridor where Roma girls

made eyes at my friend Joe, with his thick red braid
and heavy rings on every finger. We climbed
the spire of the church and looked over the city

with its fairytale bridges spanning the river.
I broke my shoes navigating and had to buy
red leather slides; Marcela insisted. New York,

Mumbai, Merida the beautiful—I was the one
who mapped the infinite plan, carrying
my broken heart as an offering, plotting

a peregrination across the globe. Me, the girl
with the guidebook, the pamphlet maps
of every neighborhood, my purpose

to shoulder the leaden hours back and forth
until my knees buckled, making it look like light work—
me, the lost one, the rose of the winds, the compass.

Portrait of Dija as St. James

I.

At the northern border of Spain, D wakes
to sunrise, lying quiet for a minute. Enric's
still sleeping between two trees, his fine-boned face

her first human sight of the day. Even in sleep
he palms his scallop shell. She sneaks
her fingers to hers, tracing the ribs to their neat

origin. Their rays, she thinks, mimic the risen
sun, shot through clouds in the Pyrenees,
her four-weeks' home. But home's not what she calls

any single place these days: New York, Mallorca,
California, all home, all not home. This dawn
will serve for a while, its pink and orange aura

a blessing, a peace. It's all peregrination
anyway: like her namesake Khadija's caravan,
D's paths follow a wandering plan.

But this morning's meditations
unlace themselves from her obligations,
and she yawns, stretches, loosens the tendons

in her ankles, tight from bicycling in the mountains.
She teases knots from her short hair, scans
the track of today's ride in her guide, hops down

from her perch. "*Buenos dias*, Enric,"
she grins. He groans, throws the closest stick
at her, but she's already untied her hammock.

II.

"So what might make me cross the line," she says,
"is this notion of redemption. I was raised
with rules for judgment: if you steal, you lose

a hand. Adultery: you'll be stoned to death.
As for me, being a lesbian, I'd be stoned and then
buried in sand. No way of coming back from

that. Yet in Catholic doctrine, you can sin
and be forgiven, sin and be forgiven again.
I wouldn't have to be perfect, only repentant."

"But in many religions, we have the last judgment,
no?" asks Enric, passing her the bread.
"And doesn't the Lord resurrect even those turned to iron?"

"We all have two angels guarding us, yes,"
D admits, slicing a hunk of cheese, "but on this
earth, we're marked forever, visible to those

around us as transgressors." She sighs.
Taking her lunch in hand, she chews,
passes the water to Enric, who's

plotting their trail on laminated maps spread out
on the hard ground. He smiles. "You know, it's not
as if we Catholics have got it all right.

Cariña, there's no comfortable spot
for us gays in any religion. We have to plot
our own courses, follow our own stars."

III.

Under the Basque dark, D's not sleeping.
Light from the star-riddled sky is keeping
her attention, her eyes wide open. Not weeping

but sighing, not drowning, but waving, she prays
to a God she doesn't know how to name:
Allah, the Holy Spirit, YHWH,

in all the religions He's the same. But how
to call that wisdom up? Enric's asleep just now,
and she's alone with her confusions. No

allegiances, no illusions, just a soul in pain:
the muscle twinges from the bike trail
secondary to her chronic heartache.

Lord, have mercy on me, she mouths,
then twists her hands into a wreath,
staring at the sky. St. James's body was unearthed,

she knows, beneath a star that revealed
its message for the faithful on this road.
Compostela: the star above the field.

Yet this night is dark, the stars no clearer
one from another, and no light makes her
path more sure. Of course the bikers

know which trail to ride, but where can she
go to find her own way? "Help me
to be good," she prays. "Grant me humility."

IV.

In an old story, St. James's body was ferried
from the Middle East to Galicia, carried
back to his mission, and lost in the waves

only to wash ashore immaculate and mailed
with an armor of scallop shells. Another legend
claims a man and horse rode out toward

the ship that bore poor James's body back,
and horse and rider slipped under the dark
engulfing bay. Though those on shore expected

sure demise, horse and man rose up crowned
with scallops, baptized, not drowned.
These stories passed from believer to believer down

through centuries. Now D's reading them
in a well-thumbed guidebook, mixed in
with practical advice for what to bring

(a canteen, a stone to lay at the Iron Cross
in Foncebadon, good walking shoes)
and local lore, like the miracle St. James

bestowed on a prisoner condemned to death:
after his parents returned from their quest
to Santiago, the judge promised

to lift the sentence if the cock and hen
roasted on his plate would crow. As one,
they cackled, and saved the thankful man.

V.

In Foncebadon, it's not what she had imagined,
more like a spot on the road than a village,
and the Iron Cross very tall on a mountain of stones.

Also unlike the rest of the trip, they're surrounded
by other pilgrims who approach the growing mound
one by one, praying, most without a sound.

A nun in grey fishes through her bag for a pebble.
A boy with backpackers' dreads drops a granite chip.
D watches at a distance. Enric steps

up to the cross and lays his agate down.
D's got two rocks in hand, one sharp and brown,
her own, and a white quartz that's come

all the way from Brooklyn, where a friend asked her
to bring it on her behalf. A year of disaster—
a miscarriage, her brother in a bicycle accident—

and of course she isn't able to make the Camino.
D's happy to carry her friend's memento,
to take the burden for a while for another, too.

Easy to read the hand-written prayer on the paper;
easy to lay the smooth-edged quartz there.
But when it's time to lay her stone, she falters,

wondering exactly what she's come here for.
She can't decide which language to pray in, which prayer.
"Forgive me for what I have failed to do," she says.

VI.

After weeks of riding, D's grown lean,
her muscles often in pain, but strong,
her tricky hip less often tricky, her arms

so defined the veins bulge under her skin.
In her hammock at the end of the day, a thin
slice of moon allows the light to skim

her tan lines, a narrative marked on her flesh.
How little, she thinks, we really need. Plush
body, you served me in the life before, flushed

at times with wine, lax and loose,
and now each kilometer drops more of the kilos
I used to carry. The spirit too—how much

we think we ought to prove, to show
our worth in the eyes of others—and now
I have no need beyond a friend, a true

word or two, food and shelter for the night.
She turns to peek at Enric, turned tight
in his hammock, fast asleep, she thought,

and he asks, "Cariña, are you all right?" Smiling,
she nods, then reaches across the divide
to find his hand in the dark. "Just thinking

how lucky I am you asked me to come,"
she says, "and how much I still have to learn,"
and Enric laughs and kisses her palm.

Portrait of Greta as St. Elizabeth

1.

In mid-January, Greta picked me up
in her truck to take my broken Baby Jesus
to the Moore St. Market, where I had heard

a woman owned a stall where statues
could be repaired. My poor infant,
60 years old, maybe, had stiff wires

where his fingers ought to be.
Though sweet-faced, he flaked,
paint chipping from his cheeks, his body.

I knew that broken saints could be interred
in the crypt below our church, but hoped
he might have new life. Greta helped me out

of the truck, my pregnant belly pushing
against the plaster baby, and we were met
by three men, who inquired about the statue

wrapped in an old bath towel. Friendly,
they smelled faintly of beer. "I can
fix that for you," one said, wrenching

a wire so the plaster cracked. "I'll get
back to you if I can't find the lady inside,"
I said. "Are you sisters?" one queried.

"Yes," Greta replied. Among the fruit stalls
and the botanica, we found the lady, her stall
packed with small Infants, robes of satin

and velvet, and Tupperware tubs of acrylic
and thread. She held my Christ gently,
turning him, checking his paint. She opened

a bottle, tested it against his skin,
then promised to return him whole
within the week, so he would be ready

to present at the church on February 2nd.
Greta and I went for coffee, warming
our hands on the paper cups. "I know

I lied," she said, "and I know
they were kind, but sometimes it's best
when men ask if you're sisters to just say yes."

2.

A week later, Greta and Dija arrived
at my hospital room, Dija carrying sandwiches
in a paper bag, and my infant Christ

wrapped up in a towel in Greta's arms.
In a week, he'd turned from Italian
to Mexican, his skin now terra cotta,

long eyelashes arching above his eyes.
And his fingers had returned immaculate,
re-formed with plaster, each nail

and fingertip complete. His white shift
was edged in gold, his mouth rosebud
pink. "You look great, Susan," Greta said,

though I'd lost twenty pounds in a night,
my cheeks in high color with the effects
of extreme hypertension. "The baby's upstairs,"

Josh said, "but she can't have visitors."
And we ate the sandwiches they had brought,
good whole-grain bread, sprouts, turkey, tomato,

like manna after the hospital food. My Jesus
found a spot in the windowsill, next to the fishbowl
of chrysanthemums and Gerbera daisies.

Greta sat quietly, listening, her eyes, when
I caught them, watching mine. She gathered
the used napkins and wrappers from my bed,

and they left to let me rest. And on February 2nd,
when I was released, I carried Christ home
in my lap while our infant slept in her isolette.

Gerard Manley Hopkins
Looks at a Cloud

On his back, under a sea of stirring wisps,
Hopkins tries to find words for the cirrus,
the cumulus, the nimbostratus, the drifting crowd
of clouds like steam opening the sky. He has risen
early, wakeful from nightmares, unable to rest
though he lay in bed for what seemed like hours
as he did not sleep. Hunting that haunting,
he wrung the last dark from the night. The dawn,
grey and heavy like the Irish day, has him now,
a gnarled root torn from its bed
and tossed onto the dung-pile. His waking
is raw with rubbed nerve, with wanting
a friend. There is no human friend. There is none.

And he lies on his spine as he could not do
in sleep, turning to the stratosphere, particularizing
each feather and eyebrow of cloud, thinking
what do I recognize there? The round clouds
like eggs in an anthill roll slowly, without effort,
across the sky, moving as if they are not
moving, almost still. He thinks of his heaviness,
his own bones a weight he must strive to stir.
He thinks of the clouds' massive heft like the flesh
of the sky, a musculature sure and simple,
striated, spare, and strange: he is lifted then too,
all sinew and soul thrilled in the high reaches
of Christ's clutches, to whom all things
are light, and lifted, and lifting.

Portrait of Salvador as Don Quijote

"*Cada ocho días,*" says Clementina when I ask her
about how often Salvador goes to church. She calls him

Viejito, my little old man. Chayo calls him *el inge,*
the engineer. His sons call him *jefe,* the boss. And

when he was young, he was known as *El Caballero
Cristiano de Coyoacán,* because Salvador

was born in that neighborhood in Mexico City
named after coyotes. All over the apartment, Quijotes

drape their gangly arms and legs or stand ramrod straight
under the marvelous and damaged helmet of Mambrino

(really just a barber's basin made of brass.) And Salvador
when I meet him is not unlike them: a trim, kind-faced man

with grey hair and a neat beard, who has a way
of tilting his head down to the left and smiling. He holds

both my hands in his, gripping them firmly, and calls me
Doña Susanita. Two weeks later, I return from Taxco

with a three-inch crucifix, a walnut cross with a sterling Christ
hanging on it. He keeps it at his bedside for years.

*   *   *

Years later, a guest in their modest weekend home,
I wake before Salvador and Clementina, who like

their private time together, morning and night.
In the bright sun of Yautepec, with bougainvillea

purple and fuchsia in the yard, I hang the hammock
between the porch posts and lie, thinking about writing,

thinking about the effort it always takes for my brain
to re-enter the Spanish language, the words that escaped

yesterday and the day before, words I know, but which don't
come to mind when called. Tilting at windmills—

and Salvador's left his English workbook on the table,
learning all over again the nouns and verbs he learned

to work in London when young, so he can carry on
a conversation with his son's new American wife.

The lesson is on the conditional: *Begin each sentence with
"I wish."* And as I read, the words begin to blur: .

*I wish our politicians were honest. I wish our police
were not corrupt. I wish all the children of our country*

had enough food to eat. A list of unsolvable problems,
a blasted moor full of windmills: and then

after so many prayers for the public welfare,
a final request: *I wish my son would stop smoking.*

The Angel of Conscience

Dear Ms. Brooks, what do you do
when the ignorant come knocking to plague you?

I remember, child, that the heart is enough:
it is formed out of some inflammable stuff,
so if the ignorant come to learn,
I will not burn.

And Ms. Brooks, when you see injustice succeed
how do you not bleed?

We all bleed, my child, if one man is cut,
but a scant cup of heart's-blood is not much to let
since the Lord our God was bound in chains
to father the blood in all of our veins.

Now, Ms. Brooks, when you see the innocent die
how do you not cry?

When my children are killed, and the gun
is not sorry, I do not cry. I weep.
And yet in weeping I wake, as I should.
Our world is too much asleep.

III.

LOVE

Diptych of Two Charleses as St. Irene and St. Sebastian

I.

In a corner of the living room, a glass-and-bronze pitcher
stands on its taloned foot. Its iridescent rose and purple

gleam under a skim of dust. It's the same one
you see in the portrait of Charles on the wall: an image

painted in the eighties by another Charles,
his *semblable*, his *frère*. My Charles is here. Today

he is rounder than those gaunt days, no longer gazing
in hunger. Today, instead, he is slicing steak

to feed me for dinner. His hands are steady;
they do not shake as he balances asparagus on a knife

to transfer to my plate. I have learned for years
his particulars: he loves Sontag, hates being seated

at a restaurant without a choice of table, always wears
the double-profile cameo ring his mother gave his father.

The two faces, one white, one black, face the same direction.
The ring fits his pinky finger. His hands do not shake,

though he tells me that Charles the painter has had
a terrible break, was found wandering barefoot outside Atlanta

miles from home, carrying his cat. *Summer is always hard
for Charles,* he says. *I begged him not to leave New York.*

II.

In winter, my Charles and the other Charles and I
meet at the Guggenheim on a day so cold even fur-lined gloves

don't keep my hands warm. Charles the painter arrives
looking like a modern dandy: motorcycle boots, voluminous

pants tucked into them, a leather jacket. Kandinsky's
whole oeuvre unfolds before us, and we agree

that the monumental paintings on display ought not to have
those ghastly gold frames—something matte, white or black,

would be better. We linger in the curves of the gallery.
I tell both Charleses about the Bauhaus home I visited

where Klee and Kandinsky lived: *Klee's side was all squares
and angles, but Kandinsky brought his own furniture, antique
       wardrobes,*

overstuffed chairs. Charles the painter spots a periwinkle shade: sighs
I'd love a silk scarf in that color. My Charles, unusually subdued,

smiles and squeezes my hand, and I can tell that he is tired,
but the paintings go on for hours, each more beautiful

than the other. Near the top of the spiral, we find
the crowning jewel of the exhibition: *Several Circles,*

a map of the universe in blues, pinks, black, red, gold,
and purple. At its center, the largest circle deepens to a dark

iris, like an eye that enters the viewer's gaze. I say so.
Where have you been hiding her? Charles asks Charles. He turns

to me. *You're brilliant. You think just like me!* And the three
of us sink into contemplation of the colors: within us,

the superimposed circles rising and floating, trapped
beneath our ribs like wounds that heal themselves.

Portrait of Clementina as St. Dymphna

The-place-of-broken-rocks, the-place-of-copper,
Tepoztlán almost doesn't count as a town,

so small that when we enter a street we must
turn the car again to let another car out. Clementina

drives, wanting to show me around. Somber
and patient, she waits while I buy strings

of *papel picado* outside the market, then hosts me
at a *taqueria* where we crowd elbow to elbow.

We pass through the door in the convent wall
and enter the sanctum's cool air, dipping our fingers

in the font. The church's silence rings like a bell
as Clementina tells me the recent death in the family

was a suicide. Her husband's brother had lived
here, on a ridge of hill, with his wife and children, now

all grown. *We do not blame ourselves or him,* she says. *We
only feel very sad.* She leads me up the stairs to the halls

where monks painted arabesques in red on the plastered
ceilings. At the corner of the building, a balcony opens

south and west: to one side, the little houses, and
to the other, the green mountain topped with pyramids

that Tepoztlán faces. She points out the fenced-in
villa where he lived and the courtyard his wife

filled with aloes. We survey them together, leaning
into each other. *You always come when we need to see you;*

always when we are suffering, you are here, she murmurs,
and I can't tell whether she's addressing me or God.

Portrait of Francisco as
St. John the Baptist

In the Amate bookstore, I'm scoping out
the fiction section when a man enters:

loose shirt, sun-scorched skin, his long hair
and beard wild, as if crusted with mud or honey.

In the market, you can buy sandwich bags
of grasshoppers peppered with chili powder,

but this fellow feeds on locusts, almost
a desert creature himself. I've seen him before,

crouched in a windowsill, holding a tiny
bat like a leathery mask over his eyes.

My friend continues talking. I can't listen.
I'm staring, half-afraid he'll look my way.

That gaze might blister, or worse, see through
the cage of my ribs to the heart,

and either sear it with a brand, or squeeze
until my own blood seeps from his pores.

Father Santo *In Persona Christi*

After Mass, as we descend the church steps, a long line
of parishioners stops and starts, clasping the Father's hand.
Santo gives condolences, blesses a rosary, asks about sisters,
husbands, cousins, winks and smiles. In front of me,
I recognize a couple: the man our tithe collector, always
dressed finely in a suit, and his wife, who I remember once
in Easter season teased Santo for forgetting our Alleluias
at the end of Mass, then sang them with him on the sidewalk.
"Give us a blessing, Father. Our anniversary is tomorrow,"
she says, and he spreads his arms wide to gather them in,
palms raised. "Lord, bless this couple in their long marriage,
for their good example as partners, parents, grandparents,
living as you have taught them to do. Make their union happy
all the days of their lives," Santo says, then shakes their hands.
Between them their 4-year-old granddaughter holds out
her arms, but when Santo takes her small fingers in his,
she frowns, and raises her whole self to stand on tiptoes,
not satisfied until he crouches to give her a proper hug.

Portrait of Greg as St. Bonaventure

Fifteen years after I left his course, I find a note taped
to the office door: *Class is over at 2:50. I'll see you*

here at 3. Greg's grown older, more silver in his hair,
but the same kind face beams at me over the desk.

On the walls above his head, paintings hang, marked
and scratched with the words of his poems, some

doubled, some larger than the words around them.
"St. Francis," he muses: "when Giotto painted

those frescoes, why didn't he include the scene
when Francis kissed the leper? Previously, he was

just a rich playboy, and that day he did what he never
thought he could do, extending that fellow-feeling

to a suffering person. I've never understood how
Giotto could exclude the moment of his conversion."

He takes a call. I wander through the books on his shelf,
peruse again the old photograph of Greg with his arm

around his own teacher, now dead, the smiles on their faces
full of joy despite the weight of the past, the slap

of memory still stinging their cheeks. He puts down
the phone. "I remember you wrote then about tobacco,"

he says, time not having dulled his recollection, and I feel shame
at all the student poems I've written on and forgotten.

"That was my wife," he says, "coming to pick me up,"
and we wander to the parking lot, where a car pulls in

and a labrador leaps out, shaking a corona of river
into the air. Greg grabs her scruff and rubs the longing face,

then introduces me to his wife and daughter, and they find
their places in the car and wave as I begin my walk to dinner.

Portrait of Jess as St. Lucy

In her study, Jess leans back in a blue chair,
calves resting on the wooden desk, laptop
in her lap. In the story she's finishing,

the narrator lives in Jess's apartment, wrestles
with Japanese knotweed in the yard, and senses
the isolation of objects: a single stranded boot,

a salt shaker separated from its pepper. Jess
has known since she was a child these orphans:
they call to her, begging for completion.

Yet her own self's full of excesses that need
to be cut away or cleft. She's got to decide
which of them to keep, as in her sentences.

To wit: which should stay—jellyfish, chatroom,
coldcock, platform? And in a suitcase,
how many pairs of socks, how many books?

On a chain, which charm: sailor hat, ship's wheel,
treasure chest? The world's full of things that need
sorting, so she pushes her glasses up and bends

to the keys. In the evening, she shakes up a jar
of tequila steeped in rhubarb, froths an egg white,
rims my glass with piquin salt, and I bank

the fire with year-old newspapers so we can sit
up late. Wielding my needle-nose pliers, I add
to her necklace an anchor and a heart embossed

with a swordfish leaping over a blue enamel sea.
Across the living room, she removes
her glasses, rubs her face, and I see her through

a haze, lifting a tray. I know it's just a trick
of smoke, our dinner leftovers on a plate, but
for a minute I could swear she's offering up her eyes.

Portrait of Trent as
St. Ignatius of Loyola

Week 4 of the retreat, Trent limps across
campus sidewalks, aiming for the spire of Pip and Jim's,
his cowboy hat making a circle of shade

under which his face radiates. Noon-bells
toll for Mass. "That's the Church: stinks and clinks!
smells and bells!" he laughs. He breaks

into a whistle, finessing Bob Wills'
"When It's Honeysuckle Time In The Valley, Sally."
At the church door, a man in shabby clothes

begs alms, and out comes a fistful of change.
When we enter, Trent crosses and blesses
himself and me, then goes down on one knee

all the way to the floor, solemn, his strong brow
knit and chin lifted slightly. Incense, as promised,
wafts over us as we kneel to pray.

Unschooled, I watch Trent for the signs
of what to do: stand now, cross yourself. The priest,
white-haired, Irish, intones, "I know why

you have come today. You come to know
the truth. You come for peace. And you come
to share in God's love." The eucharistic ministers stand up,

and I notice the smooth untroubled face
of the youngest—he has Down Syndrome
like my brother. "A good guy," Trent says,

sotto voce. The priest moves his hands to form
the blessing over the bread and wine. "Jesus said,
I leave you peace, my peace I give you. Let us share

a sign of God's peace with one another." And
turning in the pew, instead of shaking hands,
Trent wraps me up in a hug.

Portrait of LB as St. Scholastica

In Greenport, in her 1890's farmhouse,
LB has a filing drawer labeled *FEARS*.

Inside it, press-on claws, a rubber mask
of a wolf's face, but no indication of the 7 years

she spent in the hospital, in surgery,
diminishing in flesh but not in spirit.

Spirited, slender as a whippet,
she's quick to link our condition

to the bestiary, deer locked in mating
struggle, mole in the sights of

the all-seeing owl. She's lived at the edge
of biology for so long she ought to have

a Ph.D. Her gentle laugh rustles
like wind in the underbrush,

her brushes with death a means
to learn more, quickening.

She tells me she doesn't expect to live
forever, or even much longer,

her voice level and even, except
for the note of doubt when she explains

she's not settled the details of her estate,
the house she wants to leave to

her brother's children, or maybe
as an artist's retreat, space for sisters

to return in peace and write.
In her living room, surrounded by globes

and old books, she glows with a certain
vulnerability, the way you'd imagine

an element would display its own corona,
its half-life. Yet she opens a drawer

marked *WISHES* and removes
a paper box, its lid labeled in French

LOTO DES FLEURS, jeux educatifs,
and writes on a slip of paper

which she places inside, and gives it
to me, who deserves a wish far less than she.

Self-Portrait as St. Edith Stein

From the train window, I watched my sisters' white palms
waving as long as I could see them. Pale roses for the Queen
of Heaven filled the cabin, headed with me to Cologne.

At home, my mother did not appear in the window to wave,
though we would not see each other again. The knowledge
of her disapproval lumped in my stomach like hard bread.

Weeks ago, when I had to face the grille and sing, I quailed.
I was more terrified to sing that hymn to Mary than when
I lectured to a crowd of a thousand students, but God

soothed me. Though shy, I did not strike a single sour note.
Weeks later, when I returned from my final visit home,
the Sisters received me kindly with white chrysanthemums

and buttoned me into my bridal gown, crowned with tulle.
We all marry our beloved Christ, and our habits frame every
expectant face. Now I have many sisters, Jewish and Christian,

and though we do not always understand each other,
God grant me the patience and love to speak well
so that I can translate between two mother tongues.

Portrait of My Father as
St. Joseph the Worker

In my father's hand, the roof planks
are only the length of his thumb.

He taps the tacks lightly to set them
in place: three rows of planks

for the front of the roof, three rows
for the back. The roof itself he hinges

with a piece of caramel leather,
as he hinges the front walls. This house

is my father's house, made again
for me. He grew up in such a cabin,

the floorboards, the sleeping loft,
the fireplace with a mantel where he hangs

just the tip of a birthday-cake
candle. He paints the chinking

between the logs on each wall, using
the child's paintbrushes he has taken

from my room. The little house
is supposed to be a secret,

but I find it under a towel
on the workbench in the basement.

When my father discovers that I have
discovered it, he takes me down

and shows me how to unclasp
the front wall, swing open the doors,

and lift the roof back to play
inside it. He shows me how he built

a chimney from dozens of flat pebbles
he found in the stream, setting them

one by one with glue. He places the ladder
so that the dolls can climb

into the loft to sleep. I hold his roughened thumb
in my fist and wonder: how lucky I am

to have a father who creates
such things with his own hands.

Portrait of My Brother as
St. Michael Archangel

A camel or a dog may lead this procession
of villagers under the Met's Christmas tree.
We'd be able to see better if the lamps were on,

but just as we arrive in the hall, they shut down
on my brother and me. Doesn't matter. All day
we've held hands while I carried my magnifying glass,

a cartoon monocle we held up to the cases
to get a bead on small things: agate intaglios,
slices of millefiore canes, Etruscan gold pearled

into encrusted earrings. In the Greek
and Roman mezzanine, clay women looked on
while Michael named the animals. When I asked

what do you see? he spoke: *horse, sheep.* If I asked him
to say cow, he bellowed MOO. Buddhist Taras,
Benin bronze, the flat-foreheaded statues

of Peru floated past my brother's gaze. Around
the world in an afternoon, we've ended beneath
a gilded gate, squinting in the dim Medieval Wing,

trying to discern if Melchior and Balthazar
are meant to be so large compared to the monkey
at their feet. I wish the lights were on,

yet strangely, a crowd gathers deeper and deeper
around the darkened tree. "I'd go around the front,
if I were you," a guard with dreadlocks warns,

and we squeeze between the taller hordes
toward the velvet rope. At once a carol starts,
and a glow seeps from the cradle. The Christ-child's

face illuminates, and then his mother's, and then
the entire gathered congregation: Joseph,
the kings, goats, shepherds, pigs, and

angels rising the height of the magnificent tree.
I turn to see what of it my brother can see.
"Oh," he breathes, and inches closer. "*Oh*."

Portrait of Jess as St. Augustine

1.

How many months since you moved away for real
and now we're in your old backyard, the lavender
you planted overblown, the weeds you defeated

risen again, clearing out the things you left behind?
These two enameled pans you bought on our only drive
to my mother-in-law's house, empty by then,

so we could write for a week together, stay up
late, drink, visit Melville's manse. You helped me
throw holy water in every corner, helped me not

to feel haunted by her absence/presence, listened
when secretly I sang to myself in another room.
Now I'm helping you load and unload the things—

a coat rack, a worn stool—you always meant to bring
to your next life. Here's a mesh ball meant
to be filled with birdseed. Here's the childhood

of your former lover, reflecting a cloud, a little sky,
that woman now so distant you use her first and last name
to refer to her. I spent days in this backyard,

its bottles and bricks half-submerged, cradling my baby
in my lap. You left. How have I lived without you
for so long, only to see you receding again from me?

2.

And still I will do anything to be near to you
as the tattoo artist inks your thigh with a hundred marks.
Among them is the name of your new beloved,

who waits this day to see if a child will be born, to be yours,
who asks to see your new tattoo and to whom you will say no.
Here's me photographing you, promising I'll be kind

in the angle and perspective, to make you look handsome.
Here's me charming your tattoo artist with the lore
that a Hindu bride will wear her husband's initials

woven into the swirls of henna on her feet and hands,
so that he must find it there on their wedding night. How come,
my friend, I'm talking about me so much? Was your home

always and only there, on the other coast, where
you wake and rub the grit and rust of desert
from your nearsighted eyes? What, really, does any of us

know about love? Is there something for you
on that other shore that you can't learn here?
Will someone burst our deafness so that suddenly

we hear? The needle vibrates. Its buzz is like
a thousand thousand bees, turning in the side
of a blasted dripping overripe lopsided stolen pear.

Triptych of Lauren, Darrin, and Zach as the Holy Family

1.

It's hard to remember that Christ was a three-year-old too
until you see Zach, sans pants, his red-blond hair
a wild halo, shrieking past. All giggles: "*Too much!*"

he shouts, "*too much!*" and sprints into his bedroom.
Lauren smiles from the rocking chair where she's
knitting. "He's been inside all day," she says, working

her double-ended needles. Her hair, since you saw her
last, has grown to her waist, a thick tumble she's knotted
with elastic. The last time you met, Zach wasn't born

yet, but he behaves as if he's known you all his life.
"Do you want to see my marbles?" he asks, emerging
from his room. "I really like your dress." And Darrin

gives hugs to his wife and his boy, takes his bike
from the entry, and exits into Emeryville, passing under
the sign above the front door that reads *Love One Another*.

2.

On babysitting night, Zach doesn't cry when the grown-ups
leave, but brings you the nail polish, one silver, one blue.
"I want silver," he says, and sits very still while you paint

each fingernail and toe, each one so small you only touch
the brush against it. Then he wants you to paint your own
nails blue. Once they're dry, you suggest it's time for a bath.

"Would you like to take a bath with me? It's such a nice day,"
he pleads, slipping his hand into yours, so you put on
a bathing suit and pile in with the boy and thirty tub toys.

There's a chicken that works like a squirt gun, and a sheep,
and Zach wastes no time, bending his dimpled back to crouch
and fill them. You've got a cow, but it's woefully weak:

the chicken's the best, with a stream like a needle, and though
Zach begs for mercy, hopping from one foot to the other,
when you put down your squirter, he shoots you right above the eye.

3.

At the playground, Lauren's brought a bag with snacks,
which is good, since the whole party's tired from the slide,
jungle gym, and swings. All sit together and share

an orange, its peel an S you separated all in one piece
from its flesh. Zach's contemplative, trying to think whose
name begins with S. The late afternoon light scatters through

the leaves of the maple above you onto his face. Lauren
confesses she's read the entire New Testament, even the letters,
but not the Old, and yet "I'm happy to be a Jew," she says.

Gathering hats and thermos and wrappers, Lauren readies
to go. "Zach, you can choose one more thing to do,"
and he runs with his last burst of juice to the climbing wall.

Lauren follows, her hands ready to catch him
if he falls, but "That's good climbing," she tells him,
"you're doing it. Go high, Zach. Go higher. Go higher."

Communion of Saints

I. Holy Innocents

In room 3, eight boxes glow
at chest-level, approached
by nurses who float between

with towels diapers thermometers
and pink and blue striped
cotton blankets washed in dozens.

For each box a monitor registers
oxygen/heart rate/breathing/pulse
in short beeps and glancing lines

of light that thread the screens,
but the nurse says *Don't look
at the machines, look*

at the baby, so we do: mothers
and fathers hovering beside
those sterile plastic habitats,

our hands scrubbed clean
with alcohol so many times
my skin resembles a rasp.

The mothers learn each other's names:
Shula, Meryl, Alicia, Bernadette,
Cheryl who's been through the NICU

twice. Standing beside our own infants,
touching hands or ankles through the portals,
we receive the blue glow reflected

so that from a long way away
it appears our children (born
at 32 weeks, 26 weeks; 3 pounds,

2 pounds, a pound and a half)
are made only of light.

II. Roll Call

Between 7 and 8, a.m.
and p.m., the shift change displaces
the parents, and I recite

to myself the litany of names
of the ones who are keeping my child
alive: the Filipina nurses from Jersey,

round-faced Giselle, Cora, Fanny,
wise Teresa, Christina, tall Mary Ann,
short Mary Ann, and Liberty;

Mrs. Cumberbatch from Barbados
in her crown of braids, who says
in the end we will be saved, at least

those of us who have chosen to be;
quick Amy, blunt Rose; Keisha, Raquel,
and Milagros who work the desk,

Milagros who says *Don't get her started!*
She was crying like that last night;
Othelia, who laughed because

my daughter held her hand over
her ear as if to say *I'm finished*
listening to all of you;

flame-haired Cathy; Christian,
the only man; Donna, Rachel,
Anna, and the head nurse, Nori,

efficient and tiny. I think of Sandy
who told me *If that doctor doesn't call you*
by noon, I'd be on that phone by 12:01,

who bore twins of her own
to this NICU years ago. I say the names
of the doctors: Dr. Eiland,

Dr. Paley, Atakent, Calabio,
and reassuring Dr. Janice Klein.
There's Yola, who taught my husband

to change a diaper before I ever saw
my infant daughter, who peered
into our faces and proclaimed

She looks like her mother. I think
of Corazon, a Capuchin,
who slipped in from room 2

because she saw the St. Francis card
in our incubator, who prays daily
for the patients and their parents, for

all the Capuchins who've gone before,
and for all those who have no one
to pray for them. And Mila

working in this ward since the Reagan era,
who showed us how to bathe her.
On video we can still see her. Expertly

lifting my daughter in one hand,
she soothes her: *Iris, you're*
a flower. Mila who, when the ward was empty

just before midnight, told me about
her own lost pregnancy the year both of her parents
passed away. *It's good to vent the feelings,*

and *Keep praying, mommy,* she said,
and turned to bathe my daughter then,
and when Iris squalled at the sponge,

Mila announced, smiling, as if those cries
were the most ordinary thing,
The lady is upset. She is cold and wet.

A Vision: Triune Harmony

Just as I wake, before my eyes release
into the light, I hear a man's deep voice
breathing beside my ear, hushed and close.
He sings as if his throat is raw and parched.
I strain to discern the words, but as I reach
toward his music, two men join
with different voices, one cello-low,
the other choirboy-high and sweet,
in descant so the message comes three times:

I died to you. I died to you. I died for you.

IV.

PAX ET BONUM

Vespers, San Damiano

The pews only seated two. We chose one
near the back wall, and while you sat,
my knees ached against worn wood.
By the time the friars entered
with the monstrance, worshippers had filled
the small aisle. Dog-eared prayerbooks passed
hand to hand. From a battered fresco,
St. Agnes watched with her lamb. We sang,
then sat silently in adoration
while the sun crept across the wall,
evening shadows filing like pilgrims
into the olive trees below Assisi.

St. Francis and the Beggar

What fabrics were piled in the market
to sell? Kashmir shawls so finely knit
they could pass through a ring,

thin cottons colored with onion-skins
that bled purple or gold, or stiff
slub silks that softened with use;

Berber carpets dyed with turmeric
and iris root, woven through with triangles
to pierce the evil eye, or tiny frogs

at their hems, or lions' paws, or oleander,
or the calming pale tones of sheep's-wool
as a ground. Roughened fingers had

knotted their skeins, plunged wrist-deep
into vats of stinking dye, curled under
a wrinkled face to sleep when day's work

was done. Handfuls of Murano beads
were molded in furnaces, their striated bands
or cane chips fusing, to purchase these

from a bearded man at port. Donkeys
navigated market through-ways, loaded down,
to deliver them to Francesco, the son

of the fabric merchant. One day, a strange
hand, so dirty it seemed stained
by walnut shells, opened beside him

as he haggled with a buyer, and when shyly
it disappeared, Francesco left them all—the yards
of silks, the wools, carpets and furs—

and ran through the market until
he recognized the hand and pressed his alms
into it. He had not seen the whorls

and loops of those fingertips, like the careful
dotted circles of North African prints,
but he knew that no person is less worthy

than commerce: that nothing on earth is made
that is not formed by nature, and nothing
produced without human or holy labor.

The Hairshirt

When the Bishop gently scolded him for stealing,
though he only meant to rebuild the falling church,

Francesco returned the coins he had gained
by selling brocades from the family's storehouse.

His father stood over the judgment, nodding,
and received the money, sure that now his willful son

would behave, but Francesco mourned the gift
he'd given, more sure than ever of his purpose.

He pictured it clearly in his mind: he would build
not with coins, but with stones, each one begged

from a neighbor until he could set and mortar them
with his still-unblistered hands. Beneath his robes

his hairshirt bristled, the one thing he owned
that his father had not given. His soul raw

with the reproach from his father's house
and rejection of his father, he stripped down.

Remanding his clothes to their owner, he gave over
what he could not claim, because he would

no longer claim his earthly father as his own.
For a son to turn his rough cheek

away, the injury must be deep, the tear in the fabric
of his loyalty irreparable. And yet, alone

and almost naked in his hairshirt, Francesco entered
the snowy woods, a small brown figment

bound at the waist with rope, free and light-hearted,
secure in his boundless orphanage. Through

the darkened trees, blending into the underbrush,
he left a long trail of praise and thanks, singing.

Of Brother Silvester and Silver and Gold

In the giving of the gifts away in the name of Christ,
Francis urged his friars to turn all they had

to others and to return to His path bearing each
his or her own cross. Bernard gave his wealth.

Silvester, seeing silver, asked for more,
because he had given stones to repair the church,

and he took all that he might want from the lap
of Bernard, by the hand of Francis. That night

Silvester saw, instead of silver, all the gold he might
imagine, the gold of God's purpose, as a cross

that rose from Francis's mouth. His head
thrown back as the cross rose into the sky

higher than human mind could see, wider than even
the horizon, the sky gone bright with the reflection

of the precious cross risen. He woke to relinquish
all wealth, all coins to him now worth less

than a swarm of flies. Stunned. Gold-blinded.
Knowing that what rises to a height beyond our seeing

and beyond the span of our periphery, age to age,
end to end to the end of days, is more than gold. Is God.

A Swarm of Flies

The holy man told them: "You found nothing because you trust more
in your flies than in God." (For he called coins flies.)
                          St. Bonaventure, *The Life of St. Francis*

As if on carrion they gather, black and shining,
their wings a blurred transparency. Each eye is like
one hundred eyes. Its facets shift and shiver in light,

show the world in a hundred variations, each slightly
more sinister than the last. And huddled together
in a deposit they see hundreds of sinister selves, close

by necessity, not by affection. In fact they see
the birefringence of a fish as only a mirror
of their oil-slick rainbow shine, only worthy

because of its resemblance to them. Flies believe
that flies are all: creators of life, harbingers of death,
your beginning and your end only possible through

their intervention. Those are flies that leave your fingers
as you pay, and flies that set your table with flatware and meat.
You offer your children flies to eat, ladled onto

their fly-bought plates. They cluster and hum
in the small mouths and hands, spawning eggs like grains of rice
that slide down throats. Within you they grow. They become

a life you cannot escape, a life enslaved. You labor
in order to serve them, bringing home multitudes,
hoarding flies whose buzz subsumes your calm, your peace,

your marriage bed. Still you never feel you have enough
of them. But soon enough this too will pass. And when you die
those will be flies that weight your eyes.

Francis and Clare in Light

If a man and a woman can be true friends,
what might we make of these two
in late afternoon, sharing a mat laid
on the forest floor and talking? What
of the shaved head of the girl, hidden
under a hood like so many rows
of field-stubble? What about
the stone-roughened hands which
had shorn her? Hands which gestured
toward and all around her, helping
the tongue in its search for enough poetry
to express the light of the world. Though
the words did not come complete, between
this man and woman an understanding
began to burn. Were there sunflowers
upon sunflowers turning their heads
in all the fields of Umbria toward the two,
their shared love of the Lord forming
another blinding sun?

St. Francis Preaches to the Birds

My sisters, he called them, then suggested they
had taken their turn to speak, and asked them
to listen. In a group of birds, how many of us
would isolate each individual? And yet
he did, watching the quick tilt of the head,
the black eyes, the dark feathers crowning them
or ruffing their necks. He recognized the one
missing the talons of her right foot, the one
with a clipped wing. As he looked into each face
and spoke, they stopped their songs
and puffed their brown and golden underfeathers,
and settled them again. Just like you, too,
when someone gives you an honest word and look,
might stop and wait to see what else he would say,
if his message was for you, my sister, my brother.

The Relics of Francis and Clare

Light work, the spinning of yarn
from wool: shear the rough
from the lamb who followed him

like a child. Card its fibers;
roll a thin thread between
thumb and middle fingertip.

A spindle's just a plaything
made of olive wood, its dark
and honey-color bands

darkening more with the oils
from your hands as you spin
it wide into the air. You

play. This play is what God
creates all his children to do.
In joy and longing you make

two stockings. You knit the wool
you've spun fine. Your brother
does not complain but his pain

radiates in sole and arch, wrists,
the wound in his thin side. He dresses
his punctures with homemade salve

you keep in a casket, a secret.
Years ago he cut your hair. Now
you twist a long strand into the fabric

to clothe his bare feet. In his
last days you hope he will be
comforted by thoughtful deeds.

You know how he rejects
soft things, kindness a luxury
he won't permit himself, but from you

he will accept it. Knit
your stitches loose and even.
Make each stitch a prayer.

St. Francis and the Parsley

In the dark, one herb seems much like another;
thick fingers are blind to the frills and tendrils,

so the flat leaves of rosemary turn to lavender,
and dill's thin fringes are mistaken for fennel.

Cook despaired. Sent out for parsley, he could
not discern which leaves were which, and then

Francis in his sickness only wanted a little.
"I'm sorry," cook offered, his fists full and wet,

sharp bitter smells all mixed with the pungent,
the delicate overpowered by the sweet.

But in his hands were some sprigs of the herb,
early and tender, to slake that final hunger,

and Francis thanked him, saying "Look down.
Whatever we need, we only have to reach for.

We only need to lower our hands to the garden
and the garden will be delivered into our hands."

At the Tomb of St. Francis

The young priest, tall in his black robe, kneels
across the aisle. In the pew in front of us,
an elderly nun rubs the beads of her rosary.
The tomb brown stone, and so small.
No wax effigy for Francis, only a rough-hewn
slab. His four friends buried too in the corners
of the room: Fra Leone, Fra Masseo, Fra Rufino,
Fra Angelo. To live surrounded by the love
of friends, and in death lie with them always close—
this I add to his lesson on happiness, and say
pax et bonum to every monk and nun I pass.

Arrivederci, Assisi

A crown of stone set into the hilltop,
the Basilica watches the day go down.
From our hotel window I lean out

into the last minutes of Umbrian sun.
The lion's face inset into the garden wall
meditates. The fields, neatly mown,

lie in shadow. A *poverello*, I accept
these riches: the rose sky, cool night
air, a memory of a friar in a baseball cap

laughing with friends at the bus stop.
San Damiano at Vespers filled with hymns;
its ancient fresco of St. Agnes worn.

The olive-wood ring a shopkeeper gave
as a present, snug on my thumb.
The bench we shared with a grandma

as we ate *culatello* and cheese. Seeing
olives for the first time in my life
ripening on a tree. The cats, one black,

one gold-and-white who followed us
down the pilgrim's trail. The four corners
of the tomb of St. Francis, and

my husband leaving a candle there.
The butcher reading "Goodbye" from a sheet
of notebook paper. To Assisi, though

we take the train tomorrow, *buona
sera, arrivederci*, good night:
peace and all good things.

Returning from Assisi

From the train window, fields of sunflowers
pushed their faces toward the light. You and I
shared facing seats, me listening to Gregorian chant
on an iPod, you snapping photos that blurred
all those flowers to a yellow-green streak. On top
of every hill, a stone cathedral. At each station, another
death's-head warning on an electrical pole, but I felt
no fear. I had seen St. Clare's blonde curls
in a glass casket, the memory reflected in the dusty
windowpane. We had surpassed the pedestrian,
entered the unknown with a single suitcase.

EPILOGUE

The Wolf of Gubbio

Imagine yourself an old wolf: lean
and ragged, belly shrunken beneath a ribcage
as bowed as a galleon's undercarriage,

shoulders broader than your painful hips,
and paws the size of a lion's. You terrify
each living thing you encounter,

voles and rats ducking into holes, rabbits
humping their soft backs, propelled
under bushes by back legs strong as their flesh

is tender. A year of drought: the fields
blown to dust, the wild animals fled
to some place where they can scrounge

a meal. To you, the world smells
of the damp fur of groundhogs and deer,
and you hunger. Your teeth ache

with the need for slaughter. You catch
the scent of human sweat, and calculate
how low you must crouch to jump

for the throat and catch it, how snap
your jaws to crush. And yet the man
approaching you holds out his hand,

a hand which might contain (it has
before) some meat. He speaks, and though
you do not understand his words,

your fear recedes. He lays his palm
on your head, and you kneel,
your hunger now a weakness inside you,

but you feel like a dog might: calm,
as if you belong to this man. Other
humans have feared and beaten you,

which raises your own hair, but he
looks into your face, rubs his thumb
against the ridge of your snout. He

offers you some warm beef,
blood running from his fingertips,
and you eat, tearing the flesh

but careful not to bite him. When you
have licked the last juice from his fingers,
he stands to leave, and you follow

into a village where many people
stare to see you enter peacefully.
He walks with you to every house,

and at every house, an offering
to feed you: a bowl of milk, a sheep's
liver, the chewy offal of a hog.

No longer ravenous, you slowly eat your fill,
then lie on your side as children rub your fur,
making their high-pitched sounds.

For the rest of your life, you never
hunger, fed at any door you pass through,
beloved and belonging. Would you

call it a miracle if you knew
that wherever you went,
someone provided for you?

Notes on the poems

FAITH:

Reading the Hours of Catherine of Cleves/*I Believe in You* quotes from the Neil Young song by that name. If Neil Young were the patron saint of anything, I think it would be perseverance. His love of his sons with cerebral palsy, and his daughter, who has epilepsy, like him, is a lesser-known aspect of his life, but a much more important one than his musical career. Though I'm into that part, too.

St. Jude Thaddeus (San Judas Tadeo, in Spanish) is the patron saint of lost causes. I learned about him from my friend Chayo, who lives in Mexico City and Cuernavaca. Chayo sometimes refers to me as her "American daughter," an honor which I try to deserve. (Chayo is the nickname for "Maria del Rosario," Mary of the Rosary. There are so many women named after Mary in Mexico that each variation gets its own nickname.)

St. Agnes is the patron saint of virgins. My friend Angela Scannapieco is a Consecrated Virgin Living in the World, an ancient designation for women who choose to marry Christ but don't want to be nuns. This is a relatively rare thing, as you might imagine. Angela is also a third-order Franciscan; St. Francis founded the Third Order for laypeople who were married, or otherwise chose to live in secular society, rather than taking a religious vocation.

St. Cecilia is patron saint of musicians. Sister Carol Woods, a poet and my friend, is a member of the Franciscan Missionary Sisters of Assisi.

St. Jerome is the patron saint of scholars.

St. Francis of Assisi was the first person to create a living crèche at Christmas, so we owe him our tradition of home nativity scenes. This poem is in memory of +Charles William "Flynn" Hirsch, my sponsor for conversion to Catholicism, and the love of my gay life.

St. John of the Cross was a Spanish monk famous for writing devotional poems, especially a poem based on the image of the stag in the Songs of Songs. He is more famous for coining the phrase "the dark night of the soul," which is commonly misused to refer to having a rough time. It is actually more appropriately applied, in my understanding, to people who are at an advanced stage in their religious faith who suddenly and inexplicably lose sight of God. Trent Pomplun has explained to me that it is probable that Jesus, in saying these words on the cross, was singing Psalm 22 rather than crying out in agony.

St. Pascual Baylon is the patron saint of the kitchen. I am indebted to Tomie de Paola's children's book *Pascual and the Kitchen Angels* for details in this poem. Also, always, to my husband.

St. Anthony of Padua is the patron saint of lost objects. He was very devoted to Jesus and one night a brother in his order saw, through Anthony's door, that Anthony was holding the infant Christ in his arms. Statues of him usually depict him holding Christ as a baby. Father Santo Cricchio is my daughter's Godfather and a Franciscan like St. Anthony.

"Mary Flannery O'Connor and Company" owes much of its content to the essay "The King of the Birds," published in her book *Mystery and Manners*. I owe a debt for the term "boon companions" to Mary Karr. This poem is dedicated to Katie Shonk.

HOPE:

St. Rita of Cascia is the patron saint of several things, but in this instance, she is patron of healing of wounds. +Henry Menzies was a member of my parish in Brooklyn and a proud native of Belize.

Nina Simone's commitment to telling the truth about the lives of black people, and her honesty about the anger she felt about injustice, are models I think we could learn from in this particular moment in history.

St. Fiacre is the patron saint of gardeners, which I learned from an art print in Marie Ponsot's apartment. While researching him, I discovered that he was a hermit who denied entry to women approaching his property, out of a strong sense of his vow of chastity. It may be partially for this reason that my poem about Marie turned so feminine—in the sense that it is born out of a sense of her own particularly feminine strength, to nurture and to tell the truth about women's lives. Marie was my poetry teacher for 11 years, and I am thankful for every moment I spent in her classes. One of the highest compliments I ever received from a student was, "You are my Marie."

St. Roch is the patron saint of plague victims, usually depicted in the visual arts with his dog. He was the caretaker for many plague victims until he contracted the plague himself, and was exiled to the woods, where his dog brought bread to him daily until he recovered. Mark Doty is arguably the patron saint of our plague, for the attention and dignity he has brought to the stories of people with AIDS. We are in a slightly different historical moment now due to the efficacy of HIV medication, but it is easy for those of us in the United States to forget the ravages of this disease in Africa, where affordable medicine and preventive education are harder to obtain. Mark has been my beloved teacher for many years, and I am lucky to have him in my life.

St. Agatha is the patron saint of breast cancer sufferers and sexual assault survivors. She was martyred by having her breasts torn with pincers (or cut off, depending on which story you read.) She was also imprisoned in a brothel after refusing to marry the man who desired her. Fortunately, so far I have dodged a bullet, and my mammogram came back normal, though it is uncanny to see that inside your body, images can appear of fireworks and shooting stars.

St. Stephen was the first martyr of the Christian church. He is invoked against headaches, and my friend Ann Jurecic is a migraine sufferer as well as a tremendous thinker about the intersections of medicine, literature, and creativity. She has been a terrific friend and colleague to me.

St. Martin de Porres is the patron saint of doctors, barbers, and interracial harmony, also known as the St. Francis of the Americas. He was the son of a nobleman and a freed slave, and his father sponsored his education so that he could become a barber/doctor (which was essentially the same profession in Peru in the 16th century.) Evie Shockley is a poet and scholar with extraordinary grace and fierce commitment to honoring the history of African-Americans. I am lucky to have her as a friend and colleague, too. Selected phrases in this poem come from Evie's poem "My Life As China."

St. Thérèse of Lisieux died at 24 of complications from tuberculosis. She is known for her "little way" of faith, making a difference in even the smallest things we can do in service to Christ. She also said during her lifetime that she would "let fall a shower of roses" after her death. People who are devoted to her often experience roses as a sign of her attention. E. is a beloved friend who underwent punishing treatments of radiation for tonsil cancer in her early thirties.

St. Christopher is no longer considered a saint of the Roman Catholic Church, because it is not possible to historically verify his existence or the stories of him carrying both the devil and Christ across a river from bank to bank. (Not at the same time, obviously.) I prefer to maintain my devotion to the giant of a man who found the infant Christ extremely heavy to carry. Love to all my friends who spent the summer of 2001 in Prague with me, especially Katie Shonk, Marcela Sulak, and Joe Tyrer.

The Camino de Santiago is a pilgrimage path in Spain which hosts thousands of pilgrims every year. Dija Amer is my friend and the daughter of a deeply respected imam, who once shared his mosque with a Christian congregation who had lost their lease just before Christmas. I wish Dija love on her continued path—bicycling and otherwise. Details of the Camino in this poem are mostly taken from the Lonely Planet: Spain guidebook.

St. Elizabeth was the cousin of the Virgin Mary, who was also pregnant at the time of Mary's pregnancy. She is the patron saint of pregnant women. Greta Dana has been a terrific support to me during the birth of my daughter and in the years thereafter.

Gerard Manley Hopkins's weather journals were brought to my attention by Brad Leithauser's introduction to *Mortal Beauty, God's Grace*. Any fan of Hopkins will recognize the words I borrow from "God's Grandeur" here. I dedicate this poem to Father Timothy Dore.

Don Quijote is not a saint of the Roman Catholic Church, as he is a fictional character, but my friend Salvador Aguirre is associated with him forever in my mind, being a true caballero and truly a loving Christian. Mexico's corruption is widespread, often fatal, and horrifying, and yet Mexico's people have an indomitable spirit and persistence in the face of tragedy. I wrote this poem keeping in mind the 43 students disappeared in Aytozinapa in September 2014. (Spanish phrases in the poem are mostly translated on the spot, except for "cada ocho días" which means literally "every eight days," and "El Caballero Cristiano de Coyoacán" which means "the Christian Gentleman of Coyoacan.")

"The Angel of Conscience" refers to Gwendolyn Brooks. Her conviction that injustice could only be overcome by love is even more powerful considering her clear vision of that injustice. This poem is dedicated to my dear friend Raymond Shipman, who was the first to explain to me that it is Jesus' blood in all of our veins that makes us all brothers and sisters.

LOVE:

St. Sebastian is the patron saint of athletes, difficult children, and homosexuals. St. Irene is the woman who found him stuck full of arrows after he was sentenced to death for speaking out against the emperor Diocletian, and she nursed him back to health, after which he returned to insult the emperor loudly, in public, and was put to death more effectively. My two Charleses, +Charles Hirsch and Charles Bjorklund, were fast friends for decades, and interchanged these roles with each other for many years before Charles Hirsch's death. Charles the Artist has been a great comfort to me ever since my Charles died, and I now think of him as my Charles as well.

St. Dymphna is the patron saint of the mentally ill. Clementina has been one of my two mothers in Mexico, along with Chayo, for many years now.

In Oaxaca, Mexico, the Amate bookstore has a small but life-giving section of English language books. I saw Francisco Toledo there in person by accident one day. After he left, I asked the clerk if I was correct in recognizing the artist. "Yes," the clerk said, "and you are very lucky. Sometimes tourists come here and stand around for days hoping to see him, and they don't."

A priest is said to be acting *in persona Christi* when hearing confession, giving blessings, or otherwise appearing to parishioners in the role of Christ's representative. This poem is dedicated to the large and devout Correa family, always in the center section of Most Holy Trinity in Brooklyn.

St. Bonaventure was healed by St. Francis as a child and subsequently wrote his biography. Gregory Orr was my teacher at the University of Virginia and continues to be a kind and helpful friend. His own teacher, Stanley Kunitz, is the teacher in the photograph. Please see Kunitz's poem "The Portrait" and Greg's memoir *The Blessing* for context.

St. Lucy is the patron saint of writers. Jess Arndt is my boon companion until the end.

St. Ignatius of Loyola was the author of the Spiritual Exercises, a series of guided meditations on the life of Christ meant to aid spiritual pilgrims in a deepening of religious faith and purpose. Robert Trent Pomplun, a director of the Spiritual Exercises, has been my friend and unofficial spiritual director since I was 18, even though it took me almost 20 years after that to actually become a Catholic. Anything good and true about my religious devotion was influenced by him.

St. Scholastica is often invoked against storms and rain, and is the patron saint of nuns. LB Thompson is a genius who I am lucky to count as my friend, though I'm fairly certain I don't deserve her. I would like to invoke St. Scholastica against all future storms in LB's life.

Edith Stein was a Jew who converted to Catholicism in Germany during Hitler's rise to power. She was a brilliant student of Husserl and became a nun in the cloister of Discalced Carmelites in Cologne in 1933, after pressure from the government to prove Aryan ancestry. She was relocated to the Netherlands during the war and was rounded up as a Jewish convert by the Nazis after a local priest denounced Hitler from the pulpit. She and her sister Rosa died at Auschwitz; in the last days of her life, Edith Stein cared for the children of the camp. This extraordinary person took the name of Teresia Benedicta of the Cross upon conversion, and because of her, so did I. Santo Cricchio, O.F.M. Conv. bestowed this confirmation name on me, and I dedicate this poem to him.

St. Joseph the Worker is the same St. Joseph who is husband of Mary, mother of Christ. My dad will be slightly bemused to be included in a collection of poems about the saints; he thinks Catholics are responsible for the election of George W. Bush, among other atrocities. I was born on the feast day of St. Joseph, which meant that my 39th birthday was also the date of the inauguration of Pope Francis. (Best unexpected birthday present ever.)

St. Michael Archangel's name means "Who is like God?" My brother Michael is one of my most beloved companions in this life.

St. Augustine's *Confessions* provided many details for this poem, including (most importantly) the stolen pear which convinced him of original sin. I am indebted to Tom Andrews's beautiful long poem about Augustine in *Random Symmetries: The Collected Poems of Tom Andrews*. Also, perpetually, to my friend Jess.

The Holy Family is alive and well in Emeryville, California. Love to Lauren, Darrin, Zach, and Finn (who was in utero when this poem was written.)

Communion of Saints refers to the concept of the Catholic family— that all Catholics are called to be saints, whether the Church beatifies us or not. The communion of saints makes us all contemporaries, no matter what century was ours on Earth. The Holy Innocents were children under the age of 2 who were slaughtered by Herod after Jesus' birth, in an attempt to kill the future King of the Jews. Having a child in the NICU is clearly not as dire as all that, but there are some rough days in there. "Roll call" refers to the practice of calling out the names of Saints, often in song, during important holidays and events in the Roman Catholic Church. In my opinion, the NICU nurses and neonatologists of St. Luke's-Roosevelt Hospital should receive immediate sainthood.

PAX ET BONUM:

These poems were written around a pilgrimage to Assisi that my husband and I undertook in the summer of 2009, made possible by an award from the Dorothy Sargent Rosenberg Memorial Fund. Versions of these stories were influenced by Bonaventure's *Life of St. Francis, Canticle of the Creatures, The Little Flowers of St. Francis,* G. K. Chesterton's *Life of St. Francis,* and other books. "St. Francis and the Beggar" contains ethnographic details about textile designs derived from the book *Amulets: A World of Secret Powers, Charms, and Magic* by Sheila Paine. Pax et Bonum means "peace and the highest good," and is the traditional greeting of Franciscans.

Acknowledgments

Many thanks to all the people in this book, aforementioned, who have been my communion of saints. Thanks go to all my patient and thoughtful poetry teachers: Eleni Stecopoulous, Gregory Orr, Rita Dove, Eamon Grennan, Cornelius Eady, Sharon Olds, Agha Shahid Ali, Denis Donoghue, Ann Lauterbach, Robert Hollander, Anne Marie Macari, and especially Mark Doty and Marie Ponsot. I have learned so much from you. Thanks go also to the teachers who most supported my learning at UVA: Elisabeth Ladenson, Sharon Hays, and Ann Lane. Thanks to Melissa Hammerle, Russell Carmony, and E. L. Doctorow. A very, very special thanks, too, to Luther and Maurice.

Thanks to my colleagues at Rutgers University, especially to Kurt Spellmeyer and Carolyn Williams. Thanks to Evie Shockley, Ann Jurecic, Dianne Sadoff, Jess Arndt, Joanna Fuhrman, Yerra Sugarman, Caridad Svich, Sarah Heller, LB Thompson, Rhea Ramey, Leandra Cain, Anna Maron, Judy Karwowski, Angela Piggee, Zelda Ralph, Carol Spry, Derek Jablonski, Courtney Borack, Cheryl Robinson, Carol Hartman, Yehoshua November, and Alfredo Franco. Thanks to all my students, too numerous to name. And to Jerry Krasner.

Thanks to Greta Dana. Thanks to Maribel Cambil and Dija Amer. Thanks to Myles, James, and Warrie Price. Thanks to Margaret Peters Schwed and the crew at her salon. Thanks to Jackson Taylor, Bhisham Bherwani, David Corcoran, Eric McHenry, Craig Teicher, Jennifer Sears, and Arun, Meera, and Anokha Venugopal. Thanks to my classmates at NYU, classes of 2000-2002. Thanks to Anthony and Sophia Santangelo. Thanks to Mariano Aguirre and Lauri Shemaria, Chavo and Lorena, Sofia, Patricio y Luciana, Salvador Aguirre and Clementina, +Padre Luis Morfin, and mi Chayo. Thanks to Magda Campillo, Carlos Campillo, Claudia Canales, and Fidelia Guzman. Thanks to Tia Litia Perta. Thanks to Michelle Lewis.

Thanks so much to the parish and the priests at Most Holy Trinity/ St. Mary's, Brooklyn, NY: Santo Cricchio, Timothy Dore, Mietek Wilk, and Father Jamie Baca from Austin. Thanks to the Franciscan Sisters of Assisi, Sister Carol Woods, Sister Mercedes Soggiu, and Sister Annie Mbewe. Thanks to Rogelio and Flor Vega, my RCIA classmates, especially Catherine Menzies, and Joaquin.

Thanks to all the Garcias. Thanks to Roberto and Edith Martis, Jharrone Martis, and Valentino Olivo. Thanks to Eileen, Robert and Cass McKeithen. Thanks to Cousin Ron Leach. Thanks to Edy Gonzalez. Thanks to Jimmy Helvin. Thanks to Jay Rachmel, Kris, and their boys. Thanks to Kevin Wray and Cerissa Morissette, and to Raymond Shipman and his children, all growing up. Thanks to Andre Hakes and Catherine Gillespie, Gary Hakes, and Mason. Thanks to Mar Sidykh. Thanks to Lemia Bodden and Cristina Garcia.

Many thanks to the Dorothy Sargent Rosenberg Memorial Fund.

Thanks to Robert Trent Pomplun, Gary John Adler, Nick Samaras, Angelo Alaimo O'Donnell, Paul Mariani, and Mary Ann Miller. Thanks to Dana Gioia for extremely generous advisement. Thanks to Kevin Simmonds and Sibling Rivalry Press. Here's to Catholic (and spiritual) literature.

For the opportunity, thanks so, so much to Jon Sweeney and Mark Burrows, who are kind and patient people. And to all the staff at Paraclete, of course.

Thanks to my family. Special thanks to my father and my stepmother, my mother and +my stepfather, my grandparents, especially Mimi, my father-in-law and mother-in-law, my siblings and siblings-in-law, and my niece. Much love to all of you.

And finally, all my love to my sweet husband and my wild, intelligent, and beautiful daughter.

God forgive me if I forgot someone.

Poems in this book were published in the following journals and anthologies:

"Manual for the Would-Be Saint" and "The Wolf of Gubbio" in *Image*.

"A Vision" in *Spiritus*.

"Reading the Hours of Catherine of Cleves" in *ARTS*.

"Portrait of Chayo as St. Jude Thaddeus" in *Collective Brightness: LGBTIQ Poets on Faith, Religion, and Spirituality*, edited by Kevin Simmonds (Sibling Rivalry Press.)

"Self-Portrait as St. Jerome" in *The Portable Boog Reader*.

"Portrait of Sister Carol as St. Cecilia," "Portrait of E. as St. Therese of Lisieux," "Portrait of Dija on the Camino," "Portrait of Charles as St. Francis," and "Portrait of Angela as St. Agnes" in *Assisi: An Online Journal of Arts and Letters*.

"Portrait of Mr. Menzies as St. Rita of Cascia" and "Self-Portrait as St. Edith Stein" in *St. Peter's B-List: Contemporary Poems Inspired by the Saints*, edited by Mary Ann Miller (Ave Maria Press.)

"Portrait of Marie as St. Fiacre" and "Gerard Manley Hopkins Looks at a Cloud" in *Still Against War : Poems for Marie Ponsot* (Jamie Stern/ Nan Lombardi, privately printed.)

"Portrait of Mark as St. Roch" in *Voices in Italian Americana*.

Portions of "My Life as China" are quoted with permission from Evie Shockley. This poem is included in *the new black* (Wesleyan Poetry Series.)

ABOUT PARACLETE PRESS

Who We Are

Paraclete Press is a publisher of books, recordings, and DVDs on Christian spirituality. Our publishing represents a full expression of Christian belief and practice—from Catholic to Evangelical, from Protestant to Orthodox.

We are the publishing arm of the Community of Jesus, an ecumenical monastic community in the Benedictine tradition. As such, we are uniquely positioned in the marketplace without connection to a large corporation and with informal relationships to many branches and denominations of faith.

What We Are Doing

Paraclete Press Books | Paraclete publishes books that show the richness and depth of what it means to be Christian. Although Benedictine spirituality is at the heart of all that we do, we publish books that reflect the Christian experience across many cultures, time periods, and houses of worship. We publish books that nourish the vibrant life of the church and its people.

We have several different series, including the best-selling Paraclete Essentials and Paraclete Giants series of classic texts in contemporary English; Voices from the Monastery—men and women monastics writing about living a spiritual life today; award-winning poetry; best-selling gift books for children on the occasions of baptism and first communion; and the Active Prayer Series that brings creativity and liveliness to any life of prayer.

Mount Tabor Books | Paraclete's newest series, Mount Tabor Books, focuses on the arts and literature as well as liturgical worship and spirituality, and was created in conjunction with the Mount Tabor Ecumenical Centre for Art and Spirituality in Barga, Italy.

Paraclete Recordings | From Gregorian chant to contemporary American choral works, our recordings celebrate the best of sacred choral music composed through the centuries that create a space for heaven and earth to intersect. Paraclete Recordings is the record label representing the internationally acclaimed choir Gloriæ Dei Cantores, praised for their "rapt and fathomless spiritual intensity" by *American Record Guide*; the Gloriæ Dei Cantores Schola, specializing in the study and performance of Gregorian chant; and the other instrumental artists of the Arts Empowering Life Foundation.

Paraclete Press is also privileged to be the exclusive North American distributor of the recordings of the Monastic Choir of St. Peter's Abbey in Solesmes, France, long considered to be a leading authority on Gregorian chant.

Paraclete Video | Our DVDs offer spiritual help, healing, and biblical guidance for a broad range of life issues including grief and loss, marriage, forgiveness, facing death, bullying, addictions, Alzheimer's, and spiritual formation.

Learn more about us at our website:
www.paracletepress.com or phone us
toll-free at 1.800.451.5006

SCAN
TO
READ
MORE

Paraclete Poetry Anthology

ISBN 978-1-61261-906-4 | $20.00 French flaps

This anthology spans the first ten years of the poetry series at Paraclete Press. Included are poems by Phyllis Tickle, Scott Cairns, Paul Mariani, Anna Kamieńska, Fr. John-Julian, SAID, Bonnie Thurston, Greg Miller, William Woolfitt, Rami Shapiro, Thomas Lynch, Paul Quenon, and Rainer Maria Rilke.

99 Psalms
SAID

ISBN 978-1-61261-294-2 | $17.99 Paperback

SAID's 99 Psalms are poems of praise and lament, of questioning and wondering. His decision to include 99 in this collection recalls the ancient Muslim tradition that ascribes 99 names to Allah, though the "lord" whom this psalmist addresses is not bounded by this or any other religious tradition. These psalms seek to open us to the mystery of human life, warning us of the difficulties we face in our attempts to live peaceably together in the midst of our differences.

Hungry Spring and Ordinary Song
PHYLLIS TICKLE

ISBN 978-1-61261-788-6 | $18.00 Paperback

"I think that Phyllis was a poet first and foremost, before anything else. Here she has attentively gathered all of the poems she wished to preserve from the last half century. A handful of them were written in the last few years. This book should surprise a lot of people. Its honesty leaves me breathless."
—Jon M. Sweeney, editor of *Phyllis Tickle: Essential Spiritual Writings* (Orbis), and author of the biography *Phyllis Tickle* (forthcoming)

Available from most booksellers or through Paraclete Press:
www.paracletepress.com
1-800-451-5006